Woodhall Spa
Past and Present

by

Marjorie Sargeant

Photographs: Rodger Pickavance

Woodhall Spa Past and Present

Acknowledgements

Information accompanying these photographs is believed to be correct. Thanks are given to residents who supplied additional facts.

The author is grateful for helpful suggestions and encouragement given by Directors and Friends of Woodhall Spa Cottage Museum and fellow local author, Edward Mayor.

Particular thanks are given to Director of the Cottage Museum, Rodger Pickavance, for his diligence in searching through the Museum's vast photographic collection and for painstakingly providing pictures of today.

Published by Woodhall Spa Cottage Museum
Iddesleigh Road, Woodhall Spa, Lincolnshire.

Copyright 2008: Marjorie Sargeant.

All rights reserved. No part of this publication may be reproduced, stored in a retrieval system, or transmitted in any form or by any means, electronic, mechanical, photocopying, recording or otherwise without the prior permission of the copyright holders.

ISBN: 09546443-3-6

Typeset, printed and bound by
Cupit Print, The Ropewalk, 23 Louth Road, Horncastle, Lincs., LN9 5ED.
Telephone: 01507 522339, Fax: 01507 525438, www.cupits.com

Introduction

People who do not live in Lincolnshire think of it as a flat, farming county, with towns such as Skegness and Grimsby, Lincoln with its soaring Cathedral and Stamford, on the old Great North Road.

However, after a spring of water, found to be rich in minerals, especially iodine and bromine, was discovered in the 1820s, Woodhall Spa was created and gradually became well known throughout the county, country and abroad.

At this time and in the early years of the twentieth century, there was great faith in the healing power of mineral waters and people of means regularly travelled to their favourite spa. Residents of these places soon saw the financial benefits arising from wealthy visitors and hotels were built, apartments let, shops created and entertainments arranged, to attract people to their particular watering hole.

The chief attractions of Woodhall Spa appear to have been the high mineral content of the water, the pleasant country atmosphere, with strolls in the scented pinewoods and the high standard of the hotels, particularly the famous Victoria Hotel.

After the First World War, when Spa-going became less fashionable, this village continued to be a hard working, self-contained community with its own Urban District Council. There were shops, churches, a hospital, clubs, societies and sporting facilities. Annual village events, such as a Sports Day, were held and there were concerts and entertainments in the Pavilion, which, in 1922 became a cinema, later memorably named, "The Kinema in the Woods." There was also Squire Hotchkin's fine 18 hole golf course, which attracted increasing numbers of golfers, after its opening in 1905, culminating in the course achieving high ranking in the world and becoming the headquarters of the English Golf Union.

Wishing to record the present, thousands of photographs were snapped over the years by both visitors and residents, which now give a fascinating picture of the past.

One gentleman who lived here, Mr. Johnny Wield, a bath chair owner, had many hobbies and talents. One was photography and his collection of hundreds of local views, taken on glass plates and developed in his own dark room, form the basis of a vast collection of photographs in the possession of Woodhall Spa Cottage Museum, which is housed in the bungalow in which he lived.

Since the creation of Woodhall Spa, the railway has come and gone, shops have changed many times, hotels have been built and vanished, buildings have changed their function and numerous houses have been erected. However, many residents have lived here for much of their lives and visitors still arrive regularly to our hotels and camp sites, to enjoy the amenities of Jubilee Park, to visit old established shops on the Broadway and to play golf on the prestigious golf courses.

As an elderly resident said to me, "I don't know anyone who has not liked Woodhall Spa."

I hope these photographs will give a nostalgic and interesting picture of the village through the changing times of its existence.

Woodhall Spa Past and Present

Contents

The 617 Squadron Memorial	5
The Alexandra Hospital	6
The Baths	8
The Broadway	10
The Bungalow	13
Carlton's Chemist	15
Chapman's	17
Claremont Guest House	19
The Clocktower Jeweller	20
Coronation Hall	21
Dickinson's	23
Eagle Lodge Hotel	24
Firemen	26
Gladwin's	27
The Golf Course	29
The Golf Hotel	33
Humpherson's	35
Hundleby's	36
The Kinema	37
Kirkstead Bridge	39
The Mall	41
The Methodist Church	42
The Mill	43
Petwood	45
The Post Office	50
The Royal Hotel	51
Setchfield	54
The Spa Hotel	55
St. Andrew's Church	57
St. Andrew's School	58
St. Peter's Church	59
The Station	60
Stone House	62
Tattershall Road	63
The Teahouse in the Woods	65
The Victoria Hotel	67
Victoria Hotel Coach	70
Woodlands	71

Map of Woodhall Spa

Showing approximate position of features in this book in relation to page numbers.

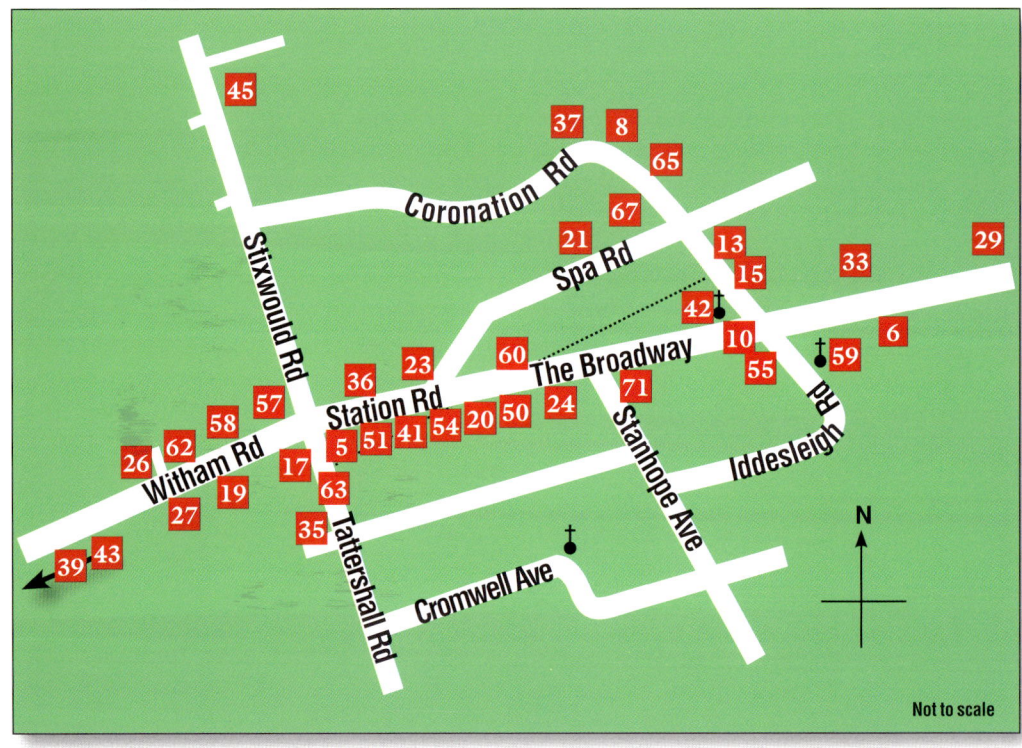

Not to scale

The 617 Squadron Memorial

Petwood Hotel, Woodhall Spa, became the Officers' Mess for R.A.F. 617 Squadron in 1943.

Because the Squadron is remembered particularly as "The Dambusters," which bombed dams in Germany to flood and therefore incapacitate the industrial area of the Ruhr, the memorial to the squadron is shaped as a breached dam. This raid took place on the night of 16th-17th May, 1943.

On the memorial is the crest and motto of the Squadron, "Apres moi le deluge." Other battles in which the Squadron took part, such as the important sinking of the German battleship, "Tirpitz," in 1944, are shown.

Names are listed of members of the Squadron from countries such as Canada, Australia, New Zealand and U.S.A. as well as Britain, who lost their lives. It makes chilling reading.

In 1987 this memorial was erected on the site of the Royal Hotel, which was itself bombed 3 months after the famous Dambuster raid. At the ceremony to mark its completion, a black Labrador appeared and walked to the front of the assembled gathering. This was uncanny as Wing Commander Guy Gibson, who commanded the raid, had such a dog, named "Nigger," which died at the time of the attack. Despite many enquiries, no-one discovered where the animal at the ceremony came from, nor to whom it belonged.

Photograph taken by Mark Upton.

The Alexandra Hospital

The Rev. J.O. Stephens of Blankney and the Syndicate of gentlemen who took over the Spa from Squire T.J.S. Hotchkin, in 1886, planned a hospital here so that poor patients could benefit from the healing water. Queen Alexandra graciously consented to give her patronage to the new hospital.

The opening day of the hospital, 29th May 1890, was a gala Day in Woodhall Spa, with flags and bunting decorating the village. The Bishop of Nottingham preached in St. Andrew's Church in the morning and then a special train arrived, bearing "distinguished persons", including Lord Brownlow, Lord Lieutenant of the County, and his wife, the Countess Brownlow who was to perform the opening ceremony at the hospital. This was conducted in the ward for gentlemen, on a raised platform, covered with a crimson cloth and "chastely decorated with flowers." After the ceremony the guests enjoyed a "sumptuous repast" at the Victoria Hotel.

Over the years the hospital was improved and considerably enlarged. It was used as a Red Cross Hospital during World War I.

After World War II it became part of the Lincoln group of hospitals, under the National Health Scheme and continued to give excellent treatment in rheumatic diseases.

However, after the disastrous collapse of the well shaft at the Spa Baths in 1983, the hospital was transferred to a ward of St. George's Hospital at Lincoln.

The Alexandra building was bought by Dr. K. Ezzat who, with his wife, ran it as a Nursing Home.

Then, in the year 2000, the company Cherry Tree Development, purchased the property and converted it into apartments. The first of these was occupied in 2002. There has since been additional building to the rear of the original hospital.

The Alexandra apartments with smart wrought iron railings.

The Baths

The discovery of Spa water was the reason for the growth of this village. Lord of the Manor, Mr. Thomas Hotchkin, erected a small bath house for private use in 1838 but as the fame of the water spread it was necessary to make many enlargements and improvements throughout the century.

Spa-going was a fashionable pursuit and visitors would know of treatments available in other places and expect to find them at this increasingly well-known "Iodine Spa."

This is a photograph of the Baths before the Syndicate took over, in 1887.

When a Syndicate of gentlemen took over the running of the establishment in 1887 a new method of raising the water, involving automatic valves, was employed, the baths were enlarged and re-modelled, under the direction of Major Davis, the architect of the watering hole of Bath and the originals became "second class baths." There were 16 first class baths, each with its "cooling room" and a dressing room where the bather could recline upon a couch, "until the fatigue of bathing wore off" and an electric bell to summon an attendant, if, by ill chance it didn't!

There were hot and cold baths, a hydraulic powered crane to lower patients into the water, "curious appliances" in which individual limbs could be suspended, needle baths, a great variety of douches, inhalation rooms, mud and massage treatments etc. It was pronounced that "the baths at Woodhall compare favourably with any in the world! They are the most perfect that can be met with."

The water was supposedly helpful for an astonishing range of ailments, from gout and arthritis to skin and nervous disorders and "women's troubles." There were tales of near cripples leaping merrily over fences after a week or two of treatment and others flinging away their crutches with gay abandon.

This is the Pump Room which was important as a meeting place where visitors could chat to each other, or read newspapers, or relax before and after treatments. They could also drink glasses of Spa water, which was generally considered to be a penance rather than a delight!

On the right is "Doctor's House" where the Medical Superintendent of the Spa lived.

Woodhall Spa Past and Present

When Spa going was less fashionable, after the Second World War, the Baths were losing money. Sir Archibald Weigall bailed them out at considerable personal cost but in the early 1920s he pointed out that this could not continue indefinitely. There were discussions about the Council taking on the responsibility but this needed government approval. Sir Archibald and Squire Stafford Hotchkin saw the Minister of Health in London and approval was granted. (It is said that Sir Archibald said the baths were necessary "washhouses"!)

Then the residents of the village had to be persuaded that this would not necessitate a large increase in the rates and there were several stormy meetings before the matter was accomplished in the autumn of 1925.

21 years later, in October 1946, Woodhall Spa Baths became a Charitable Trust.

After the National Health Service was introduced in 1948, the Baths became a centre for rheumatic diseases and developed a well respected Physiotherapy department.

Sadly, in September 1983, the top 100 feet of the well shaft dislodged and slipped 650 feet to the bottom, sending a massive force to the surface and causing immense damage to the well itself and the boilers. What was left was rapidly dismantled for reasons of safety.

Since then there have been many calls to "do something" with the premises, which are, indeed, a sad reminder of times past. The Council is working tirelessly to try and resolve the problem. We live in hope.

The Broadway

The wide, tree lined, Broadway was part of the design of Richard Adolphus Came, the London architect employed by the Syndicate who took over the Spa from Mr. Hotchkin. Mr. Came envisaged a small garden city in the midst of the flat agricultural land surrounding Woodhall Spa. The Broadway was created at the beginning of the 1890s and we can imagine it then, with horses pulling smart carriages along the straight, leafy, road while fashionably dressed visitors strolled along the pavement under the glass and wrought iron canopies in front of shop windows.

Below we see three shops of the Broadway with a black-clad and apparently unsmiling gentleman in front of each of them! (Perhaps they were brought out specially for the photo!)

Mr. Erdmann Voss, hairdresser, was one of several Germans living here before World War I. He later moved to Station Road.

Woodhall Spa Past and Present

Mackellar & Co., next door to Voss, was well patronised from Edwardian times, when as well as the expected beer, cider, spirits etc. and various European wines, the shop also advertised wine from California and Australia, "in flagons and half flagons." The next shop belonged to Mr. H.R.Maynard who was a chemist on the Broadway in the early 19th century.

The photograph below shows the same premises today. The Victorian canopies above the pavement were renovated in 2007. A ceremony was held to mark the occasion, on a fine Saturday morning in April, with children from St. Andrew's School performing Maypole dancing in the gardens of the Woodhall Spa Hotel. Afterwards they walked in procession up the Broadway, distributing posies of flowers to the shopkeepers.

This wintry scene is of the Broadway and Methodist Chapel.

Woodhall Spa Past and Present

Roger Papworth began working at this butcher's shop when still a teenager, in the summer of 1952.

At that time the business was owned by Mr. Gill, of Horncastle. There was a slaughter house on Alexandra Road.

As well as a shop entrance on the Broadway, there was a door at the back of the shop, which opened onto the station platform.

It was part of Roger's job to dash out onto the Broadway to take orders, or deliver meat, to customers in their cars. One of these was Colonel Hotchkin, who duly signed for his order, then paid his bill annually. After a while, Roger remembers him saying that he thought it would be fairer if he paid twice a year.

Roger needed to be aware of the train timetable because he was also required to hurry onto the station platform to take orders and deliver meat to customers on the trains!

He was the delivery boy of the business, taking meat, in the basket of his trusty bicycle, to houses in the area. One lady he remembers, requested firmly that the bicycle should not be wheeled into the courtyard of her garden and also said she would prefer it if he did not wear fluorescent socks when delivering to her!

Having been made Manager of the shop at the age of 18, he was taken into equal partnership by the then owner, Mr. J. Parsons of Boston, when he was 21. He has been there ever since!

The Bungalow

This building began life as a flatpack, transported to Woodhall Spa railway station and erected somewhere else! It is a corrugated iron building, made by Boulton and Paul of Norwich, who went on to manufacture aeroplanes.

Woodhall Spa Past and Present

In 1887, The Bungalow was transferred from the moor, which became the Hotchkin Golf Course, to its present site, which was next to the railway line. It became the home of Mr. Thomas Wield, who worked at the Spa Baths and began making

donkey and hand drawn bathchairs. These were used to transport patients to the Baths for treatments and also for pleasure trips around the Spa.

Mr. Johnny Wield continued his father's bathchair business but he did much else besides. Notably, he was a photographer and most of the old photographs in this book were taken by him on glass plates, which he developed in his dark room in the back garden of the bungalow.

The property has been altered over the years and has accommodated an amazing number of people as the Wield family increased. (Johnny married Asenath Dickinson, sister of the cycle and motor engineer in the village.) At one time the family even took in lodgers!

The bungalow became the property of the Cottage Museum in 1987. Since then, thousands of visitors, both local and from far away, have seen exhibits and photographs and felt the ambience of this unusual property, which was inhabited by the Wield family for over 70 years.

Carlton's Chemist

This property is listed in Kelly's Directory of Woodhall Spa, 1905, as "Carlton and Sons, Chemists, Druggists etc. Iddesleigh Road." The Spa was attracting many visitors and the position of this shop was ideal for those staying at the Victoria Hotel and for people on their way to the Baths.

This photograph shows Mr. Carlton's temporary accommodation, while the property is being built!

In 1901, Mr. Collins had come to work for Mr. Carlton and later he became the owner of the shop.

This was before large numbers of proprietary medicines were available and the chemist made up the Doctor's prescriptions and measured the correct amount into small bottles for the customer to buy.

After the death of Mr. Collins, at the end of the 1930s, Mr. Arthur Wokes, a chemist from Liverpool, bought the premises.

In the top photograph on the following page the name "Collins" is still visible above the door. Mr. Wokes was very active in village life, a member of the Parish Council, working for the provision of an ambulance for the Spa and towards the building of Coronation Hall.

However, after the decline of the Baths and the burning down of the Victoria Hotel, the shop was no longer in a good position for customers. Consequently, some years after the war, Mr. Wokes moved to premises on the Broadway, where business improved immediately and the Iddesleigh Road shop, after at least half a century, no longer belonged to a chemist.

Woodhall Spa Past and Present

The property was bought by Mr. David Waller, the well known artist, as a family home and studio.

The side of the Golf Hotel is visible at the back of the photograph.

Chapman's London and Manchester Stores, Est. 1845

Chapman's was already established in Mareham le Fen when the shop came to Woodhall Spa in the late 1880s. The shop advertised itself as a "High Class Grocer. Supplier to Boarding Houses, Clergy and Gentry." Among its "quality produce" was the mysteriously named, "Self drinking Ceylon Tea," which was sent all over the country, and bacons and hams from Denmark, Canada and Mareham le Fen! Household goods and crockery were also stocked and there was a millinery department. Older people still refer to the corner of Tattershall Road as "Chapman's Corner."

After Mr. Chapman the shop became the property of Mr. Basil Kirkby, who sold clothing. In the "Bargain Window" on the left of the top photograph overleaf, a sale is advertised.

In the middle of the 20th century, Pennington's, also a clothier's, opened in the premises, before moving to Louth.

In 1956, there was concern that the building impaired visibility for traffic on Tattershall and Witham roads and, after unsatisfactory experimentation with bollards, it was decided that the corner of the premises should be demolished. On the left of the centre photograph overleaf the "H" at the end of the name, "Achurch," is visible. This hardware shop was in Woodhall Spa from Edwardian times.

Decorative tubs, seat and the wooden frame containing a map of the village were placed on the site of the demolished building in 1997.

At one time there was a stench pipe in what is now the middle of the mini roundabout. The pole dated from when sewage was installed in the village. Sewage was a great problem in

Woodhall Spa Past and Present

Edwardian times because of the greatly increased number of people residing here in The Season. A resident remembers a gentleman making a regular inspection by lifting a manhole cover there and disappearing down a ladder for, perhaps half an hour! Decorative lamps were erected over the base of the pipe.

A roundabout was placed here as early as

April 1937 but it was not popular and was removed in July of the same year!

On the right of the photograph is the beginning of Witham Road, with advertisements for The Gun Shop, which opened in 2001 and Book Fayre, which came to Woodhall Spa in August 2005.

Claremont Guest House

In September 1888, Claremont Guest House, Woodhall Spa, run by Mrs. Sharpe, was reported in the newspaper as having 8 visitors. It was one of several boarding houses at that time.

Mrs. Claire Brennan, who with her late husband, Gerald, took over the Guest House over a century later, in May 1993, makes the point that it is, probably, the only one still operating as such today.

Proprietors of Claremont Guest House after Mrs. Sharpe, have included Mrs. Dickinson and later, Mrs. Sneath. Ladies often saw to the boarding business while their husbands continued with their own employment.

At the bottom of the drive is the coachhouse which provided a stable for the pony and with a room next to it for

the coach and coachman. Visitors could thus be conveyed to the baths for their treatment. To the left of this building is the garden of a house on Tattershall Road. This was Claremont House, the home of the Post Office, with Mr. Sharpe the Postmaster for many years.

Later in the 20th century Mr. and Mrs. Simmonds also undertook care of the elderly in Claremont, two of whom were still in residence when the business was bought by Dave and Janet Donson. They continued into the 1980s and Claremont became an established Bed and Breakfast.

A frequent visitor, who became a personal friend of Mr. and Mrs. Brennan, was a gentleman called Les Pridgeon who lived in Lincoln. He was a painter and enjoyed painting scenes of Woodhall Spa so much that he frequently cycled here, stayed at Claremont and then cycled home again. His painting of the Spa Baths in Edwardian times can be seen in the Cottage Museum.

Left: The attractive old wrought iron railings outside Claremont.

The Clocktower Jeweller

The little row of shops where this is situated is part of Woodhall's period charm.

The clock, despite its olde worlde appearance, is relatively new. In the 1980s, Earl Spencer M.V.O. D.L. and his wife, Countess Raine Spencer, toured spas of Great Britain, in her capacity as Chairman of the Spas Committee. Among well known spas visited, such as Bath and Royal Tunbridge Wells, was Woodhall Spa and this village featured in the handsome book which was produced following the tour.

While here, the Countess expressed the desire to give something to the village and it was decided that a clock would be a useful, decorative and fitting memento of the visit. The Gent clock, costing several thousand pounds, was made at the Faraday Works, Leicester and it was put in place in August 1986. Notice it has only three faces. The side which faces onto Clarence Road is black. It functions by electricity and there are precise instructions for altering the time. Apparently it takes 47 minutes to change the hour in Spring and Autumn!

This was not the first clock in the Spa. Almost a century earlier, in July 1898, the Woodhall Spa U.D.C. decided to erect one to commemorate Queen Victoria's Diamond Jubilee. (This had taken place in July of the previous year!). A 98 year old resident remembers a clock on the wall of the Council Offices, which were on Tattershall Road in the early years of the 20th century. There is mention in the "Horncastle News" in February 1921 that "the Jubilee clock has been taken down for repair." Another resident remembers a clock on the wall of Jefferies, which occupied Chapman's corner during World War II.

Dramatically, the clock stopped at the exact time the parachute mines dropped on the village in 1943.

The present jeweller took over from the previous owner in May, 2004.

Coronation Hall

At the end of World War II it was felt that a new village hall was needed. The Winter Gardens of the Royal Hotel, home to so many meetings and concerts, had been destroyed by a parachute mine in 1943.

So, in August 1946, a meeting was held and a Community Centre Committee was formed, with Mrs. Boys, wife of a local doctor, as Chairman and Mr. Woodroffe Walter, Estate Agent, Vice Chairman.

At this time of postwar shortages construction was only allowed for essential projects. There was, however, a surplus of armed forces buildings available. First, however, a site must be found and money must be raised. In the spring of 1947 the total balance of funds was £31-2-0d!

Largely through the efforts of Mrs. Flury of Petwood Hotel, a Ladies' Working Party was formed which held an American Tea and launched a fund raising quiz, so that early in 1948 funds totalled £145-16-9d. In the autumn the organisation changed its name to "Woodhall Spa Community Association" and offered membership to all residents for an annual subscription of 2/6 a year.

Over a period of time, several sites were considered;- in Victoria Avenue or Stanhope Avenue (neither of which was then completely built up) in Jubilee Park; on the site of the Winter Gardens; between the school (now Came Court) playing fields and Stixwould Road; the football field at that time adjacent to the Golf Hotel and in part of the gardens of the Victoria Hotel.

In the autumn of 1949, Mr Knowles, local builder and husband of a Committee member, showed plans for the latter site, explaining that he thought it ideal and by the end of the year planning permission was obtained.

In February 1950, the committee visited Woodhall Aerodrome at Tattershall Thorpe and saw a building which had been used for concerts and dances, which they deemed suitable.

The building at Woodhall Aerodrome which became Coronation Hall.

An application for a grant was made to the Ministry of Education, citing a total cost of £3,532 for the purchase of the building and its re erection, the land and fencing, paths etc.

Site clearing was done by volunteers, the building was dismantled and conveyed to Woodhall Spa and rebuilding was undertaken by Mr. A.F. Kirkby of Witham Road.

On 6th November 1953, five months after the coronation of Queen Elizabeth II, a grand Carnival Dance took place in the new hall. The official opening of "Coronation Hall," by the Earl of Ancaster, was in June of the following year.

Various events have been held in the hall over the years. A plot of land was leased to the Youth Club and in 1972 the hall was leased to the County Council for the remaining years of the century.

Coronation Hall stands as a testament to community spirit and the dedication of local individuals who worked for this village in the latter half of the 20th century.

This shows the recently refurbished hall in 2008.

Dickinson's

Mr. Dickinson is referred to as a "cycle agent" in 1905 but he obviously realised the potential of motor transport as it began to appear more and more in this village. In 1908, he organised what was proudly advertised as "the first ever exhibition of motor cycles in the Spa."

In June 1911, the newspaper noted that "a lady riding a motor cycle caused great excitement in this place on Tuesday!"

In 1913, there was a report that "Mr. Dickinson, Motor and Cycle Engineer, has ordered a new Napier char-a-banc, to run parties of up to 16 persons to interesting places in the neighbourhood."

Families could now enjoy a trip to the seaside "for a few shillings." In 1917, he was advertising Sunbeam cars for delivery after the war ended! In 1925 he was offering an 11.9 H.P. Morris Cowley Tourer for sale at £200. The other makes of vehicle which he sold are advertised on the windows.

This photograph was taken before 1920, as the sign post directs to the Victoria Hotel, which burned down in the spring of that year.

Laura Fowler

At the end of World War II, Mrs Fowler bought the premises next to the railway line at the top of Station Road from Mr. Roslyn, who had sold china and fancy goods. She soon had a steady clientele of customers wanting her quality clothing, especially her well made skirts and fine Scottish knitwear. She did not retire until 1980. After a few years the business was taken over by Mrs. Di Jones, who kept the name "Laura Fowler" and continued selling stylish and fashionable clothes until 2007. The bi-annual sales at the shop were eagerly anticipated in the village and beyond, for their generous price reduction in quality clothing.

The formality of clothing and serving customers changed over the years but the quality of the merchandise and beautifully dressed windows remained throughout the shop's existence.

The Eagle Lodge Hotel

Woodhall Spa Past and Present

This fine, timbered building began as a house built for the Blyton family in the 1870s. Mr. Charles Blyton was a nurseryman and florist, with land stretching up what is now Spa Road, behind the station.

In 1882, the house was converted to be an hotel and it appeared on Visitors Lists of the Spa, in the summer of that year. In 1889, there were further alterations to the "Eagle Lodge Pension Hotel." It could then accommodate 30 to 40 "invalids and visitors." The date 1889 is written on a pipe at first floor level, at the front of the building. In February 1890, a new company took over the premises and licence, which totalled £12,000.

In 1935, it was advertised for sale by auction and was said to have 37 bedrooms. However, it was withdrawn from the sale at £5,500. In the late 1960s it was purchased by the local authority to become a Home for the Elderly. However, towards the end of the twentieth century it reverted to being the "Eagle Lodge Hotel" and this is how many local residents remember it.

The group, "Hoby Hotels Ltd," purchased the hotel in 2005 and after many improvements and alterations, it became "The Woodhall Spa Hotel," in the year 2006.

In the top photograph opposite, "Eagle Lodge Hotel" is inscribed on the lamp at the side of the gate.

Firemen

Volunteer firemen have been very necessary in this village. Sparks from trains often set undergrowth alongside the railway line alight and as well as house fires, there have been serious conflagrations in the Spa's hotels.

The Urban District Council, which was formed in Woodhall Spa in 1898, was responsible for the Fire Brigade. In 1905, Mr. Gladwin, Captain of the Brigade, asked the U.D.C. for long boots for his men. Quotations were taken and after examination, hand stitched pairs at 28/- were chosen, rather than "Napoleons" at 29/-

In 1908, a message was telephoned from the Victoria Hotel to the Royal Hotel asking for a member of the Brigade to be contacted at once, as fire had broken out on the premises. This took some time and unfortunately, no horses could be procured so the fire cart had to be pushed through the village by "willing helpers." Luckily, before they arrived a messenger caught them to say the blaze had been contained.

The fire engine was housed at the back of a yard next to the shops on Witham Road.

The smart new fire station was built on the other side of Witham Road in 1983.

Firemen in 2008:-

Back row, left to right:- Messrs. J. Turner, J. Draper, A. Carter, D. Bunn, M. Hare (Crew Manager), I. Draper (Watch Manager), D. Liley (Crew Manager), C. Maplethorpe.

Front row, left to right:- Messrs. S. Quinn, R. Johnson, C. Coupland, Miss L. Kemp, Mr. A. Ward.

Gladwin's

This property was part of Humpherson's Engineering Works before becoming Gladwin's. In an advertisement of 1920, Mr. Gladwin claimed he had served customers here "for 30 years past, as manager then proprietor." As can be seen, he dealt in plumbing, lighting and heating and also sold crockery and glass. He claimed to be "a Pioneer of Cycle, Motor Car and Hardware Trade in Woodhall Spa."

The premises now.

Woodhall Spa Past and Present

It would appear that Mr. Gladwin moved from his original shop, a little way along the road to what is now V.O.C. Antiques. Indeed, the name E.H. GLADWIN is etched on the glass by the door of the shop.

Elderly residents remember Gladwin's being the precursor of Gaunt's plumbing business, where the antique shop is now. Bill Gaunt was apprenticed to Mr. Gladwin and then took over the business.

After a spell as a tearoom, the premises became V.O.C. Antiques in 1986.

The Golf Course

An Edwardian gathering at the golf course.

The first clubhouse on the 18 hole golf links.

Woodhall Spa Past and Present

Woodhall Spa's first 18 hole golf course (now named the Hotchkin Course) was opened in 1905. It was built on land given by Squire Stafford V. Hotchkin, who sought advice from top golfers of the day. In 1905, caddies went on strike, demanding an extra sixpence per round. This would be an increase of 50% bringing the amount to one shilling and sixpence! The demand was refused and the leader summarily dismissed!

The clubhouse in 1965.

2008 with new building of the English Golf Union.

The course was well regarded and achieved national fame when it hosted the English Ladies' Championship in 1926. Since then many prestigious events have been held here and the English Golf Union made Woodhall Spa its headquarters in 1995. A second course, "the Bracken" was opened in May 1997.

In 2007, "Golf Magazine U.S." voted the Hotchkin Course 53rd in the world, while "Golf World," in this country, voted it the best inland course in the United Kingdom.

Woodhall Spa Past and Present

The 4th, or Tower Green, of 1905. It is now the 3rd green because of alterations to the course.

The 3rd green now, from a slightly different position to avoid the trees which completely obscure the tower.

Woodhall Spa Past and Present

The eighteenth in early days . . .
and now.

Photographs courtesy of Mr. Richard
Latham, Director of Golf, Woodhall Spa Golf Club.

The Golf Hotel

This building, in the design of the architect R. A. Came, was erected in 1888. 8 years later it became Clevedon House Preparatory School for Boys, run by Mr. Ernest Stokoe M.A. He was the first secretary and treasurer of Woodhall Spa Golf Club and a member of the first Urban District Council in 1898. In the photograph, 8 white collared and knickerbockered boys are standing in the doorway, watched by 2 ladies at a window inside. For years after the building ceased to be a school, it was still referred to as "Stokoe's School", by elderly residents.

In 1906, the building became "Clevedon Gentlemen's Club," run by Mr. Thomas Percy Stokoe, brother of Ernest. He too was a golfer, captain and then secretary of the club. Alterations, such as the addition of a ballroom, followed and by the end of the Edwardian period, the building had become the Clevedon Hotel. It was renamed "The Golf Hotel" in 1921, Squire Stafford Hotchkin, owner of the Golf Course, having taken it over during the war, when soldiers were accommodated there.

Woodhall Spa Past and Present

The property was bought by the present owner in 2003 and the following year he set about recreating a spa in Woodhall. A well was dug in the garden to a depth of 800 feet and water was discovered which, when analysed, was found to be the same mineral content as that which had made this spa famous over a century earlier. Mr. Patel was able to buy the house next to the hotel from Mr. Hotchkin and necessary alterations to house the Aqua Sante Spa began in February, 2005. The new spa opened in October of that year.

Humpherson's

Cycling, both recreational and as a means of transport was very popular in the early 20th century. Mr. Humpherson, who is also an ironmonger and sells furnishings, is advertising several popular makes of bicycle. In addition, the notice on the side of the door advertises golf and tennis equipment. The building at the back, on the right, was the weigh house of the station.

The old railway gatehouse was demolished to make way for Budgens Supermarket. The car park is where freight wagons, which carried coal, petrol and farm implements were kept. Freight transport continued after passenger services were discontinued, finishing in 1971.

When it was known that the supermarket was coming there was concern about the new business – would the R.A. Came designed, attractive Cornwall Terrace be spoiled? Would there be a problem because of traffic? At the time, this was the most northerly Budgens store, not known to many local people.

However, a queue of customers waited outside for the store to open, at Easter, on 1st April, 1999. Two veterans of the Dambusters' Raid, Flt. Lt. Jack Patterson and Flt. Lt. Bob Knight, were invited to cut the ribbon at the opening ceremony and the queue was played in by a local jazz band "Razmajazz."

Hundleby's

This is a photograph of the very well regarded grocery shop of H. Hundleby and Co. which occupied this site for much of the 20th century. Originally, Mr. Hundleby had another shop, across the river in Martin Dales. This photograph dates from about 1920 and the gentleman in the doorway is Mr. Edward Robinson, who managed the shop for some years.

Mr. Les Chapman, who worked at Hundleby's from 1923 until his retirement, as manager, in 1974, remembers that Mr. Robinson lived "over the river" and every day his wife wrapped his hot lunch, placed it in a basket and put it on the bus to be delivered to the shop, where it was collected by the watchful employees.

The popular Janet's Tearooms replaced her Farm Shop here in the Spring of 2007. Being opposite the Dambusters'

This photograph is not dated.

Memorial, Janet has made the Squadron the theme for her decorations, including a flag which flew over Petwood when it was the 617 Squadron's Officers' Mess.

Janet recalls that one day she saw a customer who was visibly moved. She discovered that the lady was from Essex and was only calling in the Spa. She had decided to have tea and saw her brother in the long photograph of the 617 Squadron on the wall of the Tearooms. He had been killed in the Dambusters' raid.

The Kinema

The "Flicks in the Sticks," as Woodhall Spa's famous Kinema in the Woods, was dubbed by the hundreds of servicemen who crowded into it during the Second World War, is unique. It is the only cinema in the country to operate by projection from behind the screen.

The building is highly unusual. Originally constructed in the late 19th century and known as "The Barn" by local folk who used it for meetings and bazaars, it had a verandah added from which spectators could watch cricket and tennis being played in the Spa grounds. It was also used as a concert hall with well known performers coming from various cities and the London stage, in Edwardian times. Then, at the beginning of the 1920s, Sir Archibald and Lady Weigall decided that a picture house was just what Woodhall Spa needed. The Baths were not doing well and the great draw for visitors, the Victoria Hotel, had burned to the ground.

Capt. C.C. Allport was put in charge and he remained so for 53 years! The new Pavilion Cinema opened in September 1922. Unfortunately, the film expected for the gala opening night (when high prices for admission of "8d, 1/6 or 2/4 inc. tax" were charged) did not arrive, so the expectant audience enjoyed a Charlie Chaplin film instead.

These were the days of silent films and local ladies, Mrs. Tyler of the sweet shop and Miss Enderby, who played the organ in the Methodist

Chapel, were employed to play suitably atmospheric music on the piano to accompany the action. The "Talkies", or "See and Hear" films arrived in the autumn of 1930 and this was when "The Pavilion Kinema" became "The Kinema in the Woods."

The Kinema was unusual, if not unique, in having deck chairs for its most expensive seats at the front. There was often a high class clientele of customers, even including Royalty, who were staying with the Weigalls at Petwood. On one occasion, Princess Marie Louise, granddaughter of Queen Victoria, was heard to request a seat where she would not be kicked! At the back were benches, which were the cheapest seats. The nostalgic deck chairs had to be replaced in the 1950s because of safety regulations.

Mr. James Green took over the Kinema in 1973. He was able to purchase and install a Compton Kinestra Organ, which gives great delight as it emerges from under the stage in the interval of the film. The organ is played at performances by Mr. Alan Underwood, who (shades of Miss Enderby on the piano) also plays the organ in St. Peter's Church.

"Kinema Too" was opened in 1994, with the film "Four Weddings and a Funeral."

Woodhall Spa Past and Present

Kirkstead Bridge

At one time Kirkstead was not considered part of Woodhall Spa. It was a small, self contained community with as much contact with Martin Dales, across the River Witham, as with the Spa. At first the river was crossed by ferry as shown in this photograph. The white gates of Kirkstead Station and various buildings of the Great Northern Railway can be seen on the opposite bank. A siding off the railway line went into the large building on the right and at the opposite side there was a road so that horses and drays could drive in to be loaded with supplies and freight from the train.

In Sept. 1891, it was reported that a new iron bridge had been opened to the public, in place of the ferry. It was a swing bridge to allow barges, which plied up and down the river with farm and other produce, to pass. The bridge was owned by the General Northern Railway, which had Parliamentary power to levy the same toll as for the ferry crossing. It

cost 1d to walk across and a few pence more for horses and carts or drays. However, it was no longer possible for farmers and other tradesmen to have an annual contract, so several of them were now sending produce by boat.

For over 30 years the Council tried to have the toll removed and this was eventually achieved in 1938!

The railway station at Kirkstead, on the Boston to Lincoln line, was very busy. In 1922 its name was changed from Kirkstead Station to Woodhall Junction so that visitors coming to the fashionable Spa would know they had arrived.

At one time people swam in the river. In August 1911 the weather was very hot and we are told that "many bathers invaded the cooling water, morning, afternoon and night."

There were in the past, as now, many fishing competitions, when the banks were lined with hopeful fishermen. These included the prestigious all England Championship, when teams from all over the country arrived at the station on special trains.

The present bridge replaced the swing bridge in August, 1968.

The Mall

The Mall is mentioned in 1890 as the venue for a meeting to discuss the desirability of forming a Gentlemen's Social Club in the village. In the same year was the comment that "without wishing to be derogatory, the Mall was not the sort of place which a gentleman and lady would visit for the refreshment they required"! (This was stated by a representative of the Eagle Hotel, which was applying for a licence to sell alcohol!).

By 1900, the building was called "The Mall Wine Office" under Mr. Roberts, who shortly afterwards retired as manager of the Victoria Hotel.

At the beginning of the First World War there was unease about Germans working in this area, of whom there were several, mostly in the hotel trade. They were rounded up and sent packing. In the newspaper of September 1914, we read of "the sensational arrest of Mr. Hots of the Mall Tavern, Woodhall Spa." He was sent from here to authorities of the government in York.

In the top photograph a gentleman is talking to a group of three youngsters by the steps of the Mall. We note the canopy, supported by tree trunks, the Royal Hotel next door and the rough state of the road and pavement. This was taken before the shops opposite the Mall were built.

With its central position in the village, its bar and billiard room, the Mall has been a popular hostelry for over a century and has had many alterations and extensions. In 1923, Mr. Fellows installed a wireless for the benefit of his customers. In the late 20th century, when outdoor eating became popular, a patio was added next to the car park.

The Methodist Church

In 1899 a Methodist chapel was built next to the railway line, on Iddesleigh Road. A few years later it was deemed too small and a larger building was decided upon, to be built in front of it, adjacent to the Broadway. The church, with its interesting spire, unusual in Methodist chapels, was built by Mr. F. M. Thomson and Son of Louth.

Foundation stones were laid on a wild and wintry January afternoon in 1907 with whirling snowflakes accompanying the bottle of coins, local newspapers, and actual stones into the ground. However, the weather on the August weekend of the opening service was glorious. The Boys Brigade and Sunday school scholars marched behind a bugle band to the chapel, where the Superintendent Minister of the Coningsby Circuit waited on the steps, to address a large gathering which had assembled to witness the ceremonial unlocking of the doors.

Unfortunately, proceedings had to be delayed for half an hour because of the late arrival of the train bearing "prestigious persons", including the President Elect of the Methodist Conference, who was to conduct the opening service.

Notice the telegraph wires in the photograph. The telephone arrived in Woodhall Spa a year before the church was built, in May 1906.

During the Second World War, soldiers of several battalions stationed here, attended services in the chapel and crowded the building for community singing on Sunday evenings.

Congregations diminished after the war but maintenance expenses increased. When a new roof was deemed necessary it was decided that the chapel could not be sustained

After various discussions in the village the building became Fordman Systems Ltd. in February 1995.

The Mill

This mill, at the end of Mill Lane, was where the Rose family lived and worked. They were a well established business of master bakers and confectioners with whom other young village men, such as Mr. Norris, trained, before becoming bakers in their own right. They delivered daily in a horse drawn cart with the name "H. Rose and Son" prominently painted on the side. Later, they used a motor van, with "J.D. Rose, Baker and Confectioner," displayed. Bread

and rolls were taken up to the door of the house in a wicker basket then the covering cloth was lifted for the housewife to make her selection. The bakery was on the right of the picture, the "living kitchen" in the middle and the sitting room on the left.

Rose also had a shop on Station Road and catered for external events, such as Revesby Show.

Right: Mrs. Mary Wield of "The Bungalow," receiving her bread.

This photograph of 2007 shows the Mill House and the neatly tended verges of Mill Lane now, where the road turns to become Green Lane.

The bottom of the mill tower is still there, behind the hedge at the left of this photograph.

Petwood

In 1905, The Baroness von Eckhardstein, heiress of Maples Furniture store in London, decided to have a "large bungalow" built on a favourite piece of woodland, here in Woodhall Spa. She was married to an important German diplomat, a friend of the Kaiser. This marriage did not last and after the divorce the Baroness married Captain Archibald Weigall, grandson of the 11th Earl of Westmorland. The house was beautifully furnished and the Weigalls led a Society lifestyle entertaining "celebrities," aristocracy and even Royalty. Locally, they hosted an annual Cricket Week, garden parties, concerts and teas for charities and dinner parties for friends.

Above: Petwood House being built

Left: This photograph shows the house and extensive grounds of Petwood under construction. Mrs. Weigall took a great interest in the gardens, which were laid out by the well known designer, Harold Peto.

The arches shown in the photo are remembered as being covered with climbing roses.

Woodhall Spa Past and Present

Outside and entrance to the house today.

The garden at the back of the house as it was.

The same view today.

Woodhall Spa Past and Present

Edwardian elegance.

The pool in spring.

The same pool today.

Woodhall Spa Past and Present

Old photograph of rhododendrons beside the lily pond and the Atalanta Temple behind.

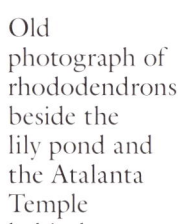

The lily pond today. The steps just visible beneath the trees are all that remain of the pretty temple.

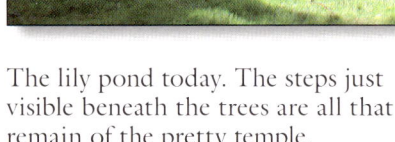

Woodhall Spa Past and Present

Past times outside the old stables.

Recent building at the hotel.

The gatehouse and old driveway.

In 1934, the Weigalls decided to leave Petwood and they persuaded London hoteliers, John and Peggy Flury, to manage it as a hotel.

The house became the Officers' Mess for R.A.F. 617 Squadron ("The Dambusters") in 1943.

The present owners have both extensively renovated the property and added to it. A grand new wing and conference centre was added in 2004. The hotel is much sought after for events and is a renowned setting for weddings.

The Post Office

The building has the crest "V.R" on the wall above the window and it was purpose built, opposite the station, at the end of the 19th century. (Queen Victoria died in 1901.) The previous Post Office was on Tattershall Road, with Mr. James Sharpe as Postmaster. He was followed, in the mid 1890s, by Mr. James Harrison Pacey. Both gentlemen served on Woodhall Spa's first Urban District Council, in 1898.

We see the Clarence Road sign on the wall and next door is "Draper, S.G. Forster." Mrs. Forster is remembered as having stocked quality ladies clothes. Mr. Forster, at the next window, sold groceries. When the telephone arrived in Woodhall Spa, in 1906, the Post Office was number 1 and Mr. and Mrs. Forster had number 2.

At one time there was a dentist, Mr. Balesford, next to Forster's and then the popular toy shop of the Misses Rose – of the bakery family – at the end.

The notice board before Forster's advises "Beware of the Trains" and of course, it is the white top of the railway gate, crossing the road, that we see in the front of the photo.

On this later photograph the solemn Victorian black railings have been painted white and there are a couple of bike stands in front of them. The post box is very noticeable and the raised red box in front of it is a stamp machine.

The Co-op, which came to Woodhall Spa in 1946, is next to the Post Office and the next window is that of the Library. Beyond them are the bungalows of Clarence Road.

Now the Library is on Station Road and the end of these buildings has been demolished to make an extended Co-op and car park.

The Royal Hydropathic Hotel and Winter Gardens

This hotel was part of the design of London architect Richard Adolphus Came to make Woodhall Spa a garden township. Beginning as a shopping mall with decorative gardens, the hotel was built upon the site in 1897. It opened with 120 rooms and suites and the pretty, glass covered Winter Gardens, with palms and ferns, covered an area of 1,000 square yards. Some years later Mr. Came discovered a new spring of Spa water, not far from his hotel and decided to build a bath-house onto the building. This was opened in November 1907. Mr. Came hoped that this, plus the Winter Gardens would attract visitors here out of the Season, when the Spa Baths themselves were closed.

The hotel did, indeed, prove popular. It was a well managed establishment with fine gardens, tennis courts and a bandstand and a decorative high water tower in the grounds.

Various functions, such as school prize-givings, dances and concerts were held in the Winter Gardens and it was a popular venue for local folk.

However, after the First World War, Spa-going was less fashionable, so the hotel was often little used. It was decided to convert some of the building into flats and in April of 1922 we

Left: This old photograph shows both sides of the Royal Hotel, with Tattershall Road on the right. The shop on the corner bears the name H. Flower, chocolatier and is advertising Cadbury's chocolate on the window. Unfortunately, in June 1891, Mr. Henry Flower

was adjudicated bankrupt with assets of £36-5-0d but liabilities of £200.

Right: This is taken looking up Station Road towards the Mall. A lady in the back of the carriage is wearing a stylish hat!

The notice on the corner of the building says Royal Hydro HOTEL & Winter Gardens..

Woodhall Spa Past and Present

read that this conversion was almost complete, with 6 flats occupied. The residents must have suffered a severe shock in May, of that year, when a bullock being taken to the slaughterhouse, having become restive on the Broadway where it was persuaded merely to examine itself for a few minutes in a shop window, after continuing on its way and reaching the Royal, crashed through a window of one of the flats.

On 17th August 1943, the Royal Hydropathic Hotel and Winter Gardens was hit by a German parachute mine and suffered much damage. It was deemed too expensive to repair and so was demolished. The site was given to the Urban District Council as a memorial to the village.

Above: This shows the Winter Gardens prepared for a function, perhaps taken from the balcony at the end of the room, where one could sit and watch proceedings below.

Right: This photograph shows the sad state of the hotel after it was bombed and demolished. The Mall, at the top, remains but damage was sustained by several shops opposite the hotel.

Woodhall Spa Past and Present

Left: The decorative water tower within the grounds of the Royal Hydro Hotel and Winter Gardens.

Below: The site as it is today with the 617 Squadron Memorial, an attractive peaceful oasis in the middle of Woodhall Spa.

Setchfield

This shop, next to the Mall, was a barber's, in pre war days.

In the photograph, Mr. Setchfield is standing in between his assistants outside the shop. The gentleman on the left was Frank Mayhew. The sign above the shop states:-

V.E.Setchfield
1st or 2nd Class
GENTLEMEN'S
HAIRDRESSING
SHAVING SALOONS

The window is full of advertisements for popular brands of cigarettes.

For much of the 20th century the shop was a butcher's and Mr. Hirst continued this tradition when he took over the premises in 2004. He and his assistant are pictured standing outside it in 2008.

The Spa Hotel

In 1888, land costing £100 and "sufficient for two houses," was bought by Mr. Oliver Cromwell, a builder from Kent, who saw business opportunities in this increasingly popular Spa village. One of these properties, "Northcote House" was bought by Dr. Robert Cuffe, recently retired from the Spa Baths, who turned it into a Sanatorium, "Northcote Hydro."

In 1907, the property was valued at £1,800 and it was bought by Mr. Alwin Gustav Goring, to be a hotel. The following year it opened as "Northcote Hotel" and soon had a substantial list of visitors published in the Visitors List of the newspaper.

Mr. Goring changed the name to "Hotel Goring" and like its, now famous, namesake in London, it flourished.

Two sides of The Spa Hotel. The lady in the doorway is wearing a frilly white pinafore.

Spa Hotel and gardens.

Woodhall Spa Past and Present

However, unlike his brother in London, German Mr. Goring had not taken out British nationality and like most Germans working in this country, he was deemed undesirable when war broke out in 1914. In March of the following year, he "surrendered the lease."

Squire S.V Hotchkin stepped into the breach, the hotel was renamed "Lawson's Hotel" and so it continued until 1921, when it was taken over by Crest Hotels and opened as "Spa Hotel."

It was a popular venue for local functions during most of the twentieth century, before being sold (for £120,000) to M. H. Marshall, builder, in 1984.

Mr. Marshall applied for permission to build several flats on the land occupied by the Hotel. 10 apartments were allowed and the hotel was demolished.

In 1988, Sealhome Ltd. offered these new properties for sale. The first apartment at "Spa Court" was occupied in 1988.

Above: The demolition of the popular hotel.

Right: Spa Court apartments at the end of the 20th century.

St. Andrew's Church

When the spa at Woodhall was still in its infancy after Squire Hotchkin built a Bath house and a small hotel in the 1830s, it was decided to erect a church. The chief mover was Rev. Edward Walter, the Rector of the parish of Langton and the chosen site was on glebe land of that parish, at what is now the crossroads of Woodhall Spa. The architect chosen was Mr. Lewin of Boston, who had designed Holy Trinity church in Horncastle and the foundation stone was laid by Sir Henry Dymoke (the King's Champion) of nearby Scrivelsby, in April 1846. The church was consecrated by Bishop Kaye, in November 1847. It is interesting that Rev. James Conway Walter, son of the motivator of the new church, was its vicar from 1869 until 1889.

Langton St. Andrew's was a prettily proportioned building, with thick stone walls. Some of the stone came from the ruins of the twelfth century priory at Stixwould. The walls inside were white, setting off the fine hammerbeam wooden vaulting, which was graced by 10 decoratively carved, hovering angels. There were sufficient pews to seat 190 worshippers. The ends of the pews were attractively carved.

As the village and the number of summer visitors grew during the nineteenth century, it became

The site of the church today.

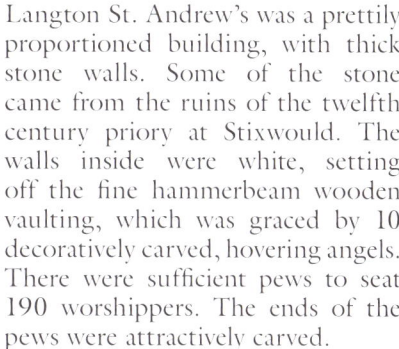

apparent that the church was too small. On occasions such as harvest, some of the congregation had to stand at the back and even in the porch!

The photograph at the top of the page shows the wall of the old vicarage, on the left.

In 1943 a parachute mine was dropped on Station Road, diagonally opposite the church and after this it was deemed unsafe. Eventually, in 1957, this attractive landmark, scene of so many local weddings, baptisms and funerals was demolished. A stone in the graveyard marks the position of the altar. The poignant graveyard remains.

St. Andrew's School

The village school was opened in 1847. It cost £226-9-6d. This was the year in which the newly built St. Andrew's Church was consecrated.

Several children from outlying districts, such as Reed's Beck, walked considerable distances, in all weather, from the age of five, to attend school. In the 19th century, the Headmaster complained that the roof was just a shell, allowing temperatures to rise to the high 80s in summer and fall to just above freezing point in winter. The building is remembered from the 1920s as having 3 rooms, one of which was partitioned and was heated by a large Tortoise stove. Classes were of mixed ages and often had over 40 pupils. On one occasion when a member of staff was absent, the Headmaster had a class of 60. However, the school seems to have been well regarded and received very good inspection reports.

In 1895, Messrs. Humpherson and Gladwin went to the school "to inspect the closets, with a view to connecting them to the main sewage system by means of sanitary troughs and a flushing tank. This will be much preferable to the zinc pan arrangement."

Until Gartree School opened at Tattershall in 1954, children who did not go to Horncastle Grammar School stayed at St. Andrew's until they were 14.

The first part of the present St. Andrew's School, which housed the Infants' Department, was declared open by the Bishop of Lincoln, Dr. Kenneth Riches, at a ceremony on 5th October 1962. It cost £17,000.

Building continued and the Junior Department was able to transfer to the new building during the last week of term before Christmas in 1968. There have been considerable additions and alterations since.

The old building has been sympathetically converted into the bungalow which fronts Came Court.

St. Peter's Church

This church was built in 1893 to accommodate the growing population and numerous visitors to the increasingly popular watering hole of Woodhall Spa. There were seats for over 500 people. It was designed by the well-regarded architect, C. Hodgson Fowler, who was responsible for several church buildings and alterations in the county.

Only the nave was completed initially and then bazaars and

garden parties were held to raise money for the chancel, which was completed in 1904.

Over the years, alterations have been made to the building and the church hall was erected at the beginning of the 1960s.

As well as Sunday Services and weekly societies, the church has been a meeting place for residents of the village at times of local and national crises and celebrations. A service for the village was held when the Titanic sank in 1912, at the end of both World Wars and at Royal deaths and coronations.

The Station

Woodhall Spa Station on a branch line between Kirkstead and Horncastle was constructed in 1855. (This was after opposition from the Canal Company, which feared loss of custom for its boats, which carried produce on the River Witham.)

The station was a success immediately. People in the Spa could travel locally to Horncastle, Boston and Lincoln, or farther afield, without having to make their way to Kirkstead Junction. It was obviously, also a benefit to visitors and numbers increased

Woodhall Spa Past and Present

significantly after the station was opened.

In 1888, it was extended to include, two platforms, with a canopy over the South side, a new passing loop, a new signal box, a waiting room, "booking hall" and a bookshop. The alterations, together with a footbridge over the line at Tattershall Road, cost £6,112-16-2d. Railway staff were instructed to salute trains and there was to be no spitting or whistling!

The narrow shoe shop at the end of the row on the Broadway now is wedge shaped because the platform ran along behind it.

It was possible to travel to London without changing trains, because a coach was unhooked and hitched onto the next train at Boston and a daily service (excepting Sundays) from King's Cross to Horncastle, was introduced in 1898.

In March of 1912, the General Northern Railway was "conferring with the Gas Company with a view to lighting the station by gas."

The trains travelled remarkably quickly. In a G.N.R. timetable of 1913, the journey of the through coach from Woodhall Spa to King's Cross took 2 hours 58 minutes and the return 3 hours 17 minutes.

In 1953 there were 5 daily passenger trains each way and a pickup goods train from Kirkstead to Horncastle but it was decided that the railway must go. After a hard fought battle with the authorities and the government, the passenger service ceased in September 1954. The last train was of 6 carriages, as sentimental last journeys were anticipated. This proved to be too long for the platform at Woodhall! However, there was an atmosphere of solemnity. Black crepe was tied around the door handles and a wreath placed on the engine, then the last train steamed out of the station.

This shows where the station was, one type of transport having made way for another. The car park is behind the Broadway and the lane continues at the top to become a leafy walk, the track of the old railway line.

Stone House

This property, "Stone House," on the corner of Witham and King Edward Roads, was the home of Mr. Basil Kirkby. He was a bespoke tailor and the fitting room was behind the window on the right of the photo and his shop, in which he sold shirts, socks etc. was on the left. It is not clear what happened in the room which has "Studio" on the window. A barber's pole juts out above the door.

The advertisement in the window is (as so often) for tobacco, cigars and cigarettes.

The people in the photograph look very prim, in their stylish hats, while a disinterested dog stares at the hedge.

When Chapman's went from the crossroads Mr. Kirkby moved his business there. Mr. Kirkby's brother, Arthur, was a builder in the village.

For many years after this the property was Slater's taxis.

Tattershall Road

Above is a fascinating photograph of Tattershall Road, looking over the crossroads and up Stixwould Road. It is evidently a fine day (there is a lady with a parasol on the left and the men are wearing boater hats.) The flags suggest a gala occasion. On the left is the shop of A. Cammack. In the 1890s Mr. Alfred Cammack advertised himself as "hairdresser...... attends ladies and gentlemen at their rooms, by appointment."

The name on each corner of the left hand building is Claremont House. This was where James Sharpe was born and where for many years in the second half of the 19th century, he is reported as being a grocer, stationer, lodging house keeper, owner of a circulating library and Postmaster! The name Sharpe is above the shop next to Mr. Cammack. Mr. Sharpe died, aged 83, in 1908, by which time the Post Office had moved to its present site on Clarence Road.

The building on the right of the photograph is the Royal Hotel, which was built in 1897. There is a board with a crown near the top of the photo.

Overleaf top is the same view today. The hotel has been replaced by Royal Square and the trees are much grown. Looking up Stixwould Road we can see Bell's Estate Agency at the cross roads, with its recently restored balustrade. The property on the left belonged to Mr. John Goodyear.

Mr. Goodyear's father set up a butchery business on Witham Road in 1890. After some years he moved round the corner to Tattershall Road, where the shop was established for many decades.

Mr. Goodyear's son, John joined him in the business and continued after his father's death. In the last decades of the 20th century he also established an antique and bric a brac business

Woodhall Spa Past and Present

and after some years he retired as a butcher and used the shop, the pavement and even his land at the side for his second hand goods! There was always a fascinating display of evocative and bizarre items from the past until he gave up the business in 2008.

The Teahouse in the Woods

Woodhall Spa Past and Present

Among the many buildings erected here in the Edwardian period, was the charmingly named and prettily constructed Teahouse in the Woods. The two ladies who ran it were daughters of a London clergyman and sisters of Dr. Williams, Superintendent of the Spa Baths. They came here every year to manage the Teahouse for the Season, until in 1913, it was reported that they had bought it outright. Looking at postcards and by all accounts, it was a delightful feature of the village, situated not far from the Broadway and on the way to the Baths. The Misses Williams were charming hostesses, wearing long, lavender coloured gowns with little muslin aprons and picture hats. Everything about the place was dainty and the delicacies served were of the highest quality.

The wooden verandah was edged by attractive, slim wooden arches and there were several rustic tables on the lawns where visitors might be joined by scurrying red squirrels scampering around the trees. The building also housed a tasteful Fancy Goods shop with some of the Misses Williams embroidery on display. There was also a lending library, as can be seen on the notice board on the left of the photograph on the previous page.

After a variety of owners in the twentieth century, the Teahouse became "Macauley's at Teahouse in the Woods" in the twenty first.

Behind the building there is a path, running alongside a stream, which stretches past the side of Petwood. It used to be a very pretty walk when Petwood grounds were visible and it is still a pleasant stroll along the side of the Bracken Golf Course.

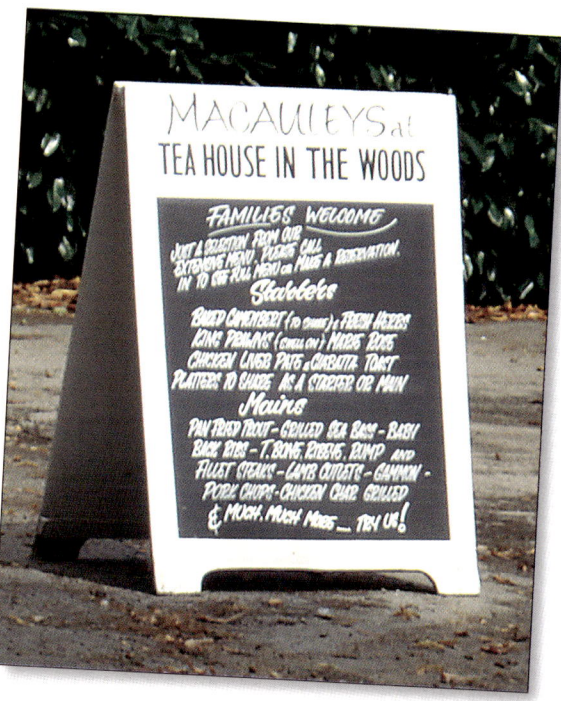

The Victoria Hotel

The splendid entrance to the Victoria Hotel.

Lord of the Manor, Thomas Hotchkin, saw the necessity of a hotel to accommodate visitors who were arriving here on hearing of the healing power of the water. His "neat and unostentatious edifice," at first referred to as the "New Hotel," or the "Spa Hotel" was completed in 1839 and named after the new Queen.

Ten years later, Mr. Hotchkin's son set about making the hotel "large and commodious, set in 100 acres." The Baths and Hotel were under the same management and in 1886 Mr. Hotchkin decided to sell the flourishing concern to a Syndicate of important gentlemen, who, in April of the following year completely reorganised the hotel's 150 rooms and added a new South Wing of 17 bedrooms with private sitting rooms. By the spring of 1888 the hotel had been "entirely remodelled and beautifully furnished throughout." There was a special inaugural day, 22nd May, 1888, to celebrate the work of the new Syndicate. Titled people, ecclesiastical dignitaries such as the Bishop of Nottingham, the Mayor of Lincoln and eminent doctors from far and near were conveyed here on a special train, graced by Lord Colville, Chairman of the Great Northern Railway.

In the Seasons that followed, the newspaper frequently reported that the hotel was "full to overflowing with admirals, generals, clergy and ladies and gentlemen of title." In the Edwardian period it cost 12/- a day for a room on the ground floor but more for a first floor room. Rooms for servants cost 2/- or 5/-.

There were frequent alterations and improvements such as in 1906, when there were new suites of rooms with balconies and a bathroom on every floor!

Woodhall Spa Past and Present

Someone at the same angle looking forlornly at the building after the fire.

The hotel had an annual turnover of £25,000 when an electrical fault in the boiler room caused a disastrous fire in the early hours of Easter Sunday morning, 4th April 1920. Staff and guests were evacuated.... fire brigades were called ....residents of the village awakened by the flames and crackling rushed to help.... guests helped to drag out furniture... the Lincoln Brigade broke down on the way.... there was insufficient water to put out the flames... someone discovered the wine cellar.... the beautiful and prestigious hotel was gutted. In modern parlance, so were the people of Woodhall Spa. It was the end of an era. The place was never the same again.

Looking up the road where the Victoria Hotel stood, towards the Pump Room. Generations of youngsters have enjoyed playing on bicycles at the "ups and downs" – the foundations of the Victoria Hotel.

New suites of rooms with balconies.

The damaged roof, after the fire.

Victoria Hotel Coach

This photograph above shows the coach of the Victoria Hotel, which was used for driving visitors to and from the station.

The gentleman on the right is the driver, Mr. George Baggaley. He is holding one of his three children who were born in consecutive years from 1905. Mr. Baggaley was a horse dealer and horse breaker, who also worked for the Weigalls at Petwood.

The house in the photo was his home, "West Cottage." It is no longer standing but was along Coronation Road.

The photograph below shows visitors at the hotel taking a drive out of the village in June 1914. Two months later World War I had begun.

Woodlands

This fine building occupies a prime site in the centre of the village. In the hey day of Woodhall Spa it was a boarding house, at one time owned by Mr. and Mrs. Hunter. She was herself a patient at the baths and was transported there by Johnny Wield in a bath chair. For a while, Woodlands was the home of Dr. Gwyn, after he lived at "Norwood" on Stixwould Road and before he built Tasburgh Lodge, at the top of Victoria Avenue. This was before the days of the National Health Service and a resident recalls his mother being ill, when he was very young. He asked if he should fetch the doctor. "Oh no," she replied. "We owe Doctor Gwyn twelve shillings and sixpence already." Dr. Gwyn died in 1922.

At the beginning of World War II Woodlands became the Infant Department of St. Andrew's School, so that the increased number of pupils, due to the arrival of evacuees from Grimsby, could be accommodated. It continued as the Infant School until after the war.

After this it became the electrical shop of Mr. Wally Cooper and then "Woodhall Electrics."

"Broadway Carpets" moved there from smaller premises on the other side of the Broadway, in 2002.

Woodhall Spa Past and Present

A resident recalls being in his car in the Broadway, in the early 1950s, when he saw a friend driving in the opposite direction. Such was the comparative emptiness of the road that they stopped, wound down their windows and enjoyed a conversation for several minutes before driving on.

Unfortunately, traffic has increased enormously since then but the Broadway of Woodhall Spa still has a wide and gracious appearance. We can imagine it a century ago, when clip-clopping horses pulled carriages bearing fashionable visitors along its shady length.